IMAGES
of Scotland

ROSYTH

HMS *Zealandia*, 1916. In March 1916, HMS *Zealandia*, a battleship of the King Edward VII class, was the first ship to pass through the entrance lock into the non-tidal basin at Rosyth Dockyard. She had met with a mishap in the Forth and is seen here entering No. 1 Dock for repairs. (Dunfermline Public Library)

IMAGES
of Scotland

ROSYTH

Compiled by
Martin Rogers

TEMPUS

First published 1999
Reprinted 2000
Copyright © Martin Rogers, 1999

Tempus Publishing Limited
The Mill, Brimscombe Port,
Stroud, Gloucestershire, GL5 2QG

ISBN 0 7524 1515 8

Typesetting and origination by
Tempus Publishing Limited
Printed in Great Britain by
Midway Clark Printing, Wiltshire

Rosyth Rent Strike, 1919. There was a great deal of unrest in Rosyth about the levels of rents charged by the Scottish National Housing Company. Although the rents had not been increased for some years, there had been a substantial reduction in the men's wages since the end of the war. Mass meetings and marches took place, including this one in July 1919 when some 3,000 people marched to the Sheriff Court in Dunfermline to support a number of residents who had been served with eviction notices. This is the dual carriageway to Dunfermline near St Leonard's, with the tram lines in the centre of the road. The strike was not successful and the rents were not reduced.

Contents

Acknowledgements

Most of the photographs used in this book have come from my own collection of postcards and photographs or have been taken by me over the last thirty-five years. To fill in gaps in my collection I have drawn on material from the Local History Collection of Dunfermline Public Library. I am very grateful for permission to use this material and should like to thank Chris Neale and the library staff for all their assistance. I should also like to thank Mrs Edith May for permission to draw on the comprehensive collection she has gathered together over the years, much of which has been deposited in the library. Without her keen interest in the photographic history of Rosyth much of this valuable material would have been lost. In the main I have carried out my own research on the information contained in the captions but I have also referred to the excellent publication *The Story of Rosyth*, produced by Inverkeithing High School and published in 1982.

I am indebted to the following bodies and individuals who have given me permission to reproduce photographs and I gratefully acknowledge their co-operation (the individual photographs are separately identified):

> Carnegie Dunfermline Trust;
> Dunfermline Press;
> Dunfermline Public Library;
> Imperial War Museum, London;
> Ministry of Defence, London (MOD);
> Norval Photographers;
> Royal Commission on the Ancient & Historical Monuments of Scotland
>   (RCAHMS);
> St Andrews University Library for material provided from the Valentine and
>   R.M. Adam Collections.

I am also grateful to the following persons who have lent me photographs for inclusion in this book: Mrs Pheme Hutchison, Miss Elspeth McKee, Mrs Winifred Mitchell, Mr John Paterson, Miss Audrie Pollard, Mrs Connie Syme, Mr Andrew Wilkie.

Where picture postcards (PPCs) have been used, I have indicated the publisher where known. Unless otherwise noted these have come from my own collection. Postcards identified as Valentine were published by James Valentine & Sons and are reproduced by kind permission of St Andrews University Library.

Introduction

In comparison with its neighbours of Dunfermline and Inverkeithing, Rosyth is a new community dating back only to 1916. However, the name Rosyth in various forms goes back to at least the early twelfth century when the Church of Rosyth is mentioned in a document by Pope Alexander III.

It is likely that Rosyth would have continued in relative obscurity if it had not been for a decision by the Government in 1903 to establish a new Naval Base there. At that time the main Royal Dockyards were situated on the south coast of England, distant from the likely threat from Germany. An east coast Dockyard was required and after some debate the site at Rosyth, or St Margaret's Hope as it was sometimes called, was selected.

Work on the Dockyard began in 1909. Although it did not have the prestige of the Forth Rail Bridge, completed some twenty years previously, it was a civil engineering project of equal significance. The plans for the Naval Base at Rosyth envisaged a substantial new community of some 30,000 people. Perhaps seeing this as a potential rival to its own position in the area, Dunfermline Town Council extended its burgh boundaries southwards to incorporate the Rosyth area.

As work on the Dockyard progressed, temporary housing accommodation was provided for the men building and (later) working in the Dockyard. This took the form of a village of huts known as 'Tin Town' or 'Bungalow City.' The need for permanent housing led to the establishment of the Scottish National Housing Company. The Garden City movement was to the fore at that time and the plans for Rosyth followed the Garden City concept with wide streets, hedges, gardens, etc. Work started in 1915 and the first houses were occupied in May 1916. Many of the bricks for the houses were manufactured at Rosyth Brickworks to the east of Park Road School and brought in by railway lines to the area later used as the Public Park.

Along with houses came the need for shops, churches, schools and places for leisure and entertainment. Many of these were initially housed in second hand wooden huts either from the Dockyard area or which had been used by the contractors building the houses in Rosyth.

In 1926 the Government reduced Rosyth Dockyard to a care and maintenance basis. The reduced fleet under the Treaty of Washington meant that there was no longer the need for all the Royal Dockyards. Many men moved back to the Southern Dockyards and a large number of houses in Rosyth fell empty. The Housing Company reduced the rents and offered the houses to people other than Admiralty employees and, as a result, the houses were occupied again fairly quickly.

After the Dockyard was virtually closed, some of its facilities were leased to Metal Industries Ltd for the breaking up of ships. Many famous ships (including German warships salvaged from Scapa Flow) ended their days in the Yard. In 1927 the Dockyard was used as a base for reserve destroyers and with relations worsening with Germany, the Dockyard was partially opened up in the late 1930s. A training establishment for boy sailors and artificer apprentices (HMS *Caledonia*) was established at Rosyth in 1937. With the declaration of war in September 1939, many men were transferred from the Southern Dockyards to bring the Dockyard up to full strength.

The period between 1926 and 1939 had been a relatively quiet time for Rosyth with little in the way of expansion or new development. The Second World War was to change all that. The need for additional housing led to the Town Council building 182 houses in the Wemyss Street/Nelson Street housing estate in 1939 and the Housing Company building about 134 houses in King's Road. In the early 1940s the Admiralty built another major housing development of 650 houses to the south of Admiralty Road. (This came to be known as 'Dollytown' because of the fairly small single storey nature of the houses which were built.) Schools were commandeered by the Forces and other buildings were used as rest centres, canteens or first aid posts. Again the Dockyard was to play an important part in the war effort.

When the war ended there were fears that the Dockyard might once again be closed. This did not happen and, indeed, the role of the Dockyard was enhanced with many of its facilities being upgraded and improved. The Burnside and Camdean areas were developed for housing in the early 1950s using some of the non-traditional forms of housing which the Government were encouraging at that time. A small estate of fifty prefabs was built in the Camdean area and a new suite of shops named 'Queens Buildings' was opened in 1956. Further houses were built in the Camdean/Primrose area in the 1960s. In the 1970s the Dollytown housing was replaced with new Council housing and the Housing Company (by then known as the Scottish Special Housing Association) developed the housing estate at Whinnyburn. At one time there was very little privately owned housing in Rosyth but this has changed considerably in recent years with the sale of Council and SSHA houses and the building of small private housing developments around Rosyth.

The early Garden City of Rosyth is still recognisable as such today, although regrettably its designation as a Conservation Area was withdrawn in 1990 by Dunfermline District Council. Rosyth's role as a Naval Base has virtually disappeared with the closure of HMS *Cochrane* and the Artificers' Training Establishment and the removal of the mine countermeasure and fishery protection vessels in November 1995. The Dockyard is still a major employer but the destinies of the town and the Dockyard are not as closely linked as they once were. Other industrial and commercial enterprises providing alternative employment have been developed in or around Rosyth and within the former Naval Base area of the Dockyard.

In this book I have set out to illustrate how Rosyth has developed over the last ninety years and some of the many changes which have taken place. I am conscious of gaps in this story partly through lack of space and partly because of the lack of suitable photographs. Photographs are an important part of our heritage and the Local History Department of Dunfermline Central Library always welcome good material for their photographic archive.

One

Early Twentieth Century

At the beginning of the twentieth century, the area we now know as Rosyth was agricultural land. The area forming the Dockyard was either part of the foreshore or was under the waters of the Forth. The railway running to the north of Rosyth was operational but there was no Rosyth Halt station. There were two road links with Dunfermline but both were narrow. The first was via the Grange Road, which continued as Brankholm Lane to Rosyth Castle and the second was via Queensferry Road which continued over Castlandhill to Inverkeithing. The only east-west links were from the Rosyth Halt area to Primrose Farm and on to Pattiesmuir and via the coast road (now known as Ferrytoll Road/Hilton Road). The farms in the Rosyth area were St Margaret's Stone, Primrose, Backmarch, Castlandhill, Orchardhead, Rosyth and Hilton. Estates to the north were Pitreavie, Middlebank and Duloch.

In this section we look at the landscape and the buildings which existed at the beginning of the twentieth century.

St Margaret's Hope, 1909. Taken from near the railway line to North Queensferry, looking west towards the Dockyard area. The sewage works now lie on the far side of the jetty (which was owned by the Tilbury Company) and the oil fuel depot in the bay further west. (Photograph by R. M. Adam, courtesy of St Andrews University Library)

Site of the Dockyard, 1909. This view is from the west side of the Dockyard site shortly after work commenced. It gives a good impression of the landscape. At the left hand side is Hilton Road and Rosyth Farm. Rosyth Castle and the Forth Rail Bridge can be seen in the distance. The huts being built are the contractors' workshops. (Dunfermline Public Library)

Rosyth Castle, c.1909. Before the Dockyard was built, the castle stood on a rocky outcrop in the Forth as this picture shows. The oldest part (the tower) dates back to the fifteenth century with later alterations and additions in the sixteenth and seventeenth centuries. It had fallen into disrepair at the turn of the century but was used at various times for storage purposes. In 1935 the building was taken into the care of the Ministry of Works (now Historic Scotland). There are plans to give improved public access as part of the Europarc proposals. (Dunfermline Public Library)

Rosyth Doocot. This lies a few hundred yards north of the castle just outside the former Dockyard boundary fence. It dates from the early sixteenth century. This photograph was taken in 1978.

Rosyth Church. To the west of the Dockyard on the outskirts of Limekilns lies the ruined church and churchyard of Rosyth. The earliest part of the church is the east gable which dates from the thirteenth century. The north wall dates from the late sixteenth or early seventeenth century. The church fell into disuse probably about the middle of the seventeenth century but the churchyard continued to be used until 1947. (Crown Copyright: RCAHMS)

Hilton Farm. This recent photograph (1994) shows the farmhouse which was built around 1825. (Crown Copyright: RCAHMS)

Orchardhead Farm, *c.1960*. This aerial view shows the farmhouse and farm steading. The north-western part of the farm steading has been used for a number of purposes over the years. In the early days it was the Dockyard Church – St Margaret's Church of England. In more recent times it was used as the Naval Married Quarters offices. The farmhouse has recently been extended and was opened in June 1999 as a residential care home.

Castlandhill House, 1910. The house was included in the Castlandhill Estate bought by the Admiralty and later became the official residence of the Admiral Superintendent of the Dockyard. (Dunfermline Public Library)

Castlandhill Farm. The farm was also included in the land purchased by the Admiralty. It continued as a farm but parts of it were used to construct concrete water reservoirs and a wireless station (see page 22) and to quarry stone used in the building of the Dockyard. This photograph by J. Wright was taken in 1958. (Dunfermline Public Library)

Seggsburn, c.1910. This group of cottages stood on the east side of Castlandhill Road opposite the entrance to the Clay Shooting range which exists today. The cottages were demolished in the early 1960s as part of the construction of the Forth Road Bridge approach roads.

Backmarch House. This was the farmhouse for Backmarch Farm and this fairly modern view (1970) shows the house when it was in use as a doctor's surgery. It was used by a succession of doctors over the years including Dr Nisbet, Dr Irvine Jones, Dr Richmond and finally Dr Currie.

Backmarch Steading. This view (also in 1970) is taken from behind the Masonic Lodge looking towards Norval Place. Over the years the main use of the buildings has been for storage purposes by the Scottish National Housing Company and its successors. The small self-contained building in the middle (which can be seen in the photograph on page 16) has had a much more varied career. It was used as a library from 1917 to 1926, as a meeting place for the Wesleyan Methodist Church until 1934 and as the headquarters for the 41st Fife Scout Group up to 1963.

Rosyth, *c.*1913. This photograph and the one opposite are part of a larger panoramic view of the Rosyth area probably taken around the autumn of 1913. These came to light only recently and for the first time we can see what the Rosyth area was like before any houses were built. The farm in the middle of the photograph is Backmarch Farm. The buildings visible are the farm steading (see page 15) with the farmhouse on the right largely hidden by trees. The building in the distance beyond the hay stacks is Wilderness Cottage (see page 18). The building at the extreme right hand edge is Pitreavie Castle (see page 20). (Dunfermline Public Library)

Rosyth, *c.*1913. The cottages in the middle of the photograph are Backmarch Farm Cottages which were situated near the Crossroads (see page 43). The buildings which are barely visible in the distance behind the cottages are Masterton Farm and the village of Masterton. Pitreavie Castle is at the left-hand edge of the photograph. (Dunfermline Public Library)

Wilderness Cottage. Originally there were two cottages on this site but in 1919 they were converted into one and extended to form Wilderness Cottage. This photograph by J. Wright was taken in 1958 after the cottage had been bought by the Methodist Church and renamed Wesley House. It was demolished in 1969 to make way for the building of the new Methodist Church which stands there today (see page 111). (Dunfermline Public Library)

Primrose Farm. The farmhouse dates from the beginning of the twentieth century and for many years was occupied by the Auchterlonie family. The farm steading was demolished in 1989-1990 (see page 125) and the former farmhouse is now surrounded by a small housing estate aptly named 'The Byres.' This photograph was taken in 1971.

St Margaret's Stone. This stood on the west side of the road to Dunfermline and is reputed to have been a resting place used by Queen Margaret in the eleventh century on her journeys between Dunfermline and the Ferry crossing. The stone was moved in 1918 when the road was made into a dual carriageway. It was moved again in 1987 to its present position on the north side of the access road into the Pitreavie Business Park near the Bank of Scotland (Visa) Centre. This photograph was taken in 1978.

St Margaret's Stone Farm. Access to the farm buildings was from the west side of the dual carriageway to Dunfermline, about 150 metres north of the present Pitreavie roundabout. The stone pillars flanking the entrance gate can still be seen. This photograph was taken in 1978.

Pitreavie Cottages, *c.*1904. The cottages were on the west side of the road to Dunfermline where the Pitreavie roundabout is now situated. They were demolished in the early 1960s to make way for the road improvements linked with the building of the Forth Road Bridge.

Pitreavie Castle. The castle dates back to the early seventeenth century with alterations in the late nineteenth century. For many years it was the home of the Beveridge family before being bought by the Air Ministry in 1938. During the Second World War it was the headquarters of 18 Group Coastal Command. An underground bunker was completed in 1941. With the formation of NATO in 1948, Pitreavie became the headquarters of the North Atlantic Area. The Castle ceased to be used by the Royal Air Force in 1995. This photograph was taken in 1974.

Two

Early Days of the Dockyard

Work started on building the Dockyard in 1909 with the main contract being awarded to the firm of Easton Gibb. The original contract was extended in various ways and at the outbreak of the First World War the Dockyard was far from ready. The non-tidal basin was brought into use in March 1916, only a matter of weeks before the Dockyard facilities were put to the test. On 31 May and 1 June the British Grand Fleet engaged the German Navy in the Battle of Jutland. The Battlecruiser Fleet based in the Forth were in the forefront of the action and a number of their ships returned to Rosyth for repairs to damage sustained in the battle. The Dockyard went on to repair and refit seventy-eight capital ships, eighty-two light cruisers and thirty-seven smaller craft during the course of the war.

Pressures on housing accommodation led to the contractors buying and erecting huts in Hilton Road for the workmen and these were erected in two phases in 1913 and 1914. Despite this housing provision, there were still a large number of men travelling to the Dockyard from the Dunfermline area. Tramlines were laid and a tram service began in May 1918. The Dockyard was virtually closed in 1926 and, up to and during the Second World War, the facilities were used to break up naval and merchant ships. The liner *Majestic* was brought to the Dockyard in 1937 to become the floating home of HMS *Caledonia* and following the outbreak of the Second World War in 1939, the Dockyard was fully re-opened.

Wireless transmitting station, 1910. At an early stage in the development of the Dockyard a wireless transmitting station and water reservoirs were built on top of Castlandhill. This view of the WT station also shows the group of houses built for the station operators.

Boathouse, 1912. Work under way on the construction of the boathouse. The electricity substation can be seen on the left. (Crown Copyright: RCAHMS)

Electricity generating station, 1912. The main electricity generating station under construction. Note the steam locomotive in the foreground. There was an extensive network of railway lines across the site for the transportation of equipment and materials. (Dunfermline Public Library)

Submarine basin, c.1913. The submarine basin (more commonly referred to as the tidal basin). The handwritten caption reads 'View looking eastwards, shewing [sic] foundation walls for intermediate jetty rendered necessary owing to deepening of basin.' (Crown Copyright: RCAHMS)

Dock No. 1, 1913. Work under way on Dock No. 1 – the first to be constructed. Note the provision for an internal caisson, which enabled the dock to be split in two. (Crown Copyright: RCAHMS)

Entrance Lock, 1915. This is the main entrance to the non-tidal basin but was also designed to serve as an additional dry dock if the need arose. Work on it was completed at the beginning of 1916 and with the dredging of the approach channel, the Dockyard was open for business. (Crown Copyright: RCAHMS)

North Wall of the non-tidal basin, 1915. Taken before the basin was flooded, this shows the entrances to the three docks. Dock No. 3 is nearest the camera. (Dunfermline Public Library)

Dockyard Workshops, 1915. Work nearing completion on the Dockyard workshops (bays). Note the use of horse transport as well as steam.

Above and below: Sunday School Concert Party, 1914. In 1913 a settlement of tin huts was erected for the men building the Dockyard. This was known as 'Tin Town' or (more grandly) 'Bungalow City.' There was a varied social life mainly centred on the Navvy Mission Church. These two photographs published in the Mission magazine were presumably taken outside the Mission hall. Mrs Burgoyne, who appears in the back row of the photograph above, was the wife of the village missionary at the time. (Dunfermline Public Library)

Bungalow City, 1914. Work under way on the second phase of Bungalow City. The road in the foreground is Hilton Road. The dark huts on the left of the photograph are in the first phase. The cottages on the roadside between the two phases are Rosyth Cottages, which were situated roughly where Brankholm Lane meets Hilton Road.

A street in Bungalow City, 1914. One of the recently completed streets in the second phase (possibly Queen Margaret Street)

Staff of Rosyth YMCA, 1915. A YMCA Naval Institute was opened in September 1915 at the corner of Ferrytoll Road and Castle Road (where the Royal Sailors' Rest or Aggie Weston's premises are now). This is the staff of the institute at that time.

HMS *Crescent* entering the Basin in 1916. The Dockyard Depot Ship, HMS *Crescent*, was the first ship to enter the non-tidal basin (through the direct entrance). (Dunfermline Public Library)

HMS *Lion*, 1916. The battlecruiser HMS *Lion* was the flagship of Vice Admiral Sir David Beatty at the Battle of Jutland. This and the next two photographs were taken shortly after the Battle of Jutland.

HMS *Princess Royal*, 1916. A battlecruiser of the Invincible Class. The netting shown was swung out on the wooden beams as a defence against torpedoes while the ship was at anchor.

HMS *Warspite* in No. 1 Dock, 1916. The battleship HMS *Warspite* was one of the ships most badly damaged in the battle. During one of the squadron's turns, *Warspite's* helm had jammed and she was hit by shells from a number of the German ships. The Dockyard workshops (or bays) can be seen in the background.

Ships in dock, 1916. This unusual view from September 1916 shows HMS *Warspite* (right) still in dock with the battleships HMS *Collingwood* (centre) and HMS *Canada (left)* in the other two docks. Note the 250-ton crane under construction on the right of the photograph.

Ceremony held in No. 3 Dock, 1916. There are a few photographs of ceremonies held in No. 3 Dock at various times but unfortunately they do not give any indication of the nature of the ceremonies. Note the Royal Marine bandsmen in the foreground. The rectangular blocks are for the ship's keel to rest on when in dry dock.

Rosyth Troop of Boy Scouts, 1916. Mr Darwin Needham succeeded Mr Burgoyne as Village Missionary and started a Boy Scout Troop in 1915. The troop were successful in the first inter-troop competition for a silver bugle, 'The Gibb Bugle', and they are pictured here with the bugle in 1916. The adults are Assistant Scoutmaster Hoff, Scoutmaster Needham and Petty Officer Roberts. The Gibb Bugle is still competed for annually by scout troops in Dunfermline District. (Photo by Norval)

Tramway track in Castle Road, 1917. Work started in 1917 on the construction of a tramway link between Dunfermline and Rosyth. It ran along what is now the grass verge on the west side of Castle Road. The temporary Church of Scotland building was to the left of where the photographer was standing. The buildings on the right were accommodation blocks etc. (Dunfermline Public Library)

Tram in front of the houses in Bungalow City, c.1920. The tram service began in May 1918 and continued until July 1937, when the Dunfermline tramway system closed down.

Inverkeithing Labour Exchange, 1921. The large number of men employed on building the Dockyard and the turnover in staff led to the opening of a Labour Exchange on the western outskirts of Inverkeithing in February 1911. This continued in existence for many years. The site now lies under the Forth Road Bridge approach roads at the Ferrytoll interchange. (Dunfermline Public Library)

North Wall of Rosyth Dockyard, 1921. In March 1918 the Government took over Easton Gibb's contract and continued the work of building the Dockyard and its facilities. The North Wall was extended to provide additional wharfage for taking on fuel and stores. It was planned to construct a breakwater parallel to the North Wall to create a second tidal basin but with the subsequent rundown and closure of the Dockyard this scheme was dropped.

Oil fuel depot, 1922. Work on constructing the oil fuel depot beside the Dockyard was completed in 1919. Thirty-seven steel tanks were constructed together with a large concrete reservoir with a capacity of some 250,000 tons of oil. This view from Rosyth Castle shows the roof of the concrete reservoir on the left with some of the tanks beside it. The reservoir was strengthened and the roof replaced in the early 1940s. Castlandhill House can be seen through the trees above the oil tanks.

Naval Stores building, 1922. In the early 1920s work began on a large Naval Stores building and it is shown here nearing completion. It became known as 'Alcatraz' and was demolished in 1998.

Wesleyan Methodist Church Choir, *c.1924*. The Army and Navy Board of the Wesleyan Methodist Church opened a church and institute in Castle Road in January 1917. This continued in use until 1926. The choir is pictured here outside the church with their minister, Rev. Louis Porri.

Constructive Drawing Office staff, 1925. The decision taken at the end of 1925 to close the Dockyard and put it on a care and maintenance basis resulted in many men having either to transfer to the Southern Dockyards or to find alternative employment. This and the following photograph were taken at the end of the year, probably as the process was about to get under way. Second from the right in the second row from the back is William Pollard.

Engineering Drawing Office staff, 1925. On the right-hand end of the back row is Walter McKee (junior). After the Dockyard closed he joined the Royal Fleet Auxiliary.

Hindenburg at Rosyth, 1930. A number of possible alternative uses were suggested for the Dockyard when it closed, most of which never materialised. One that did was shipbreaking. Metal Industries Limited leased parts of the Dockyard basin and, from time to time, the graving docks to break up merchant and naval ships. Many of the ships of the German fleet scuttled at Scapa Flow were salvaged and towed to Rosyth to be broken up. Only one, the battlecruiser *Hindenburg*, was salvaged the right way up and she is seen here arriving at Rosyth in August 1930. (Dunfermline Public Library)

A German battleship at Rosyth. This is probably the *Friedrich der Grosse* which arrived at Rosyth in August 1937. In the background is the South Arm and in the basin are destroyers of the Reserve Fleet. (Dunfermline Public Library – Douglas Cornhill Archive)

A German battleship in dry dock, *c.1937*. Again, probably the *Friedrich der Grosse*. Note the blocks to distribute her weight over the dock floor. (Dunfermline Public library – Douglas Cornhill Archive)

HMS *Caledonia* at Rosyth in 1937. The Government decided to establish a training facility in Scotland for boy entry seamen and artificer apprentices ('tiffies'). As a stop gap measure whilst shore facilities were being built, the liner *Majestic* was commissioned as HMS *Caledonia* in April 1937. With the outbreak of war in September 1939, the boy seamen were transferred to the Isle of Man and the apprentices were housed in King's Road School for about a year. (Dunfermline Public Library – Douglas Cornhill Archive)

Field gun competition, *c.1938*. The Caledonia boys engaged in many inter-divisional competitions, including a field gun competition. This is taking place on the former parade ground area to the west of No. 1 Dock. (Dunfermline Public Library – Douglas Cornhill Archive)

Three

The Garden City – Houses

Rosyth was built at a time when the Garden City Movement was to the fore. The aim was to have planned communities of about 50,000 people living in cottage type houses with gardens, extensive open spaces and protected green belts. A new body, the Scottish National Housing Company, was set up to develop Rosyth. The first batch of 150 houses were in the triangle formed by Admiralty Road, Queensferry Road and Backmarch Road, plus some houses in King's Crescent and Findlay Street. Until street names were allocated, the roads and streets were given a code. Backmarch Road, for example, was known as A1. The formal opening ceremony for the first of these houses took place in May 1916 and a house in Admiralty Road was selected for the occasion.

A contract for the second and third phases was awarded to a London Firm, Holloway Brothers, in February 1917. A railway siding was constructed from the main railway line in the Burnside area and a light railway system ran into what is now the Public Park, allowing bricks to be readily distributed to various parts of the site. In all, some 1,600 houses were built in the three year period 1915-1918. There were two later contracts – sixty houses in Leslie Road, Cromwell Road and Park Road in 1921 and forty houses in the triangle around the Baptist Church (i.e. Queensferry Road, Dick Place and Park Road) in 1924.

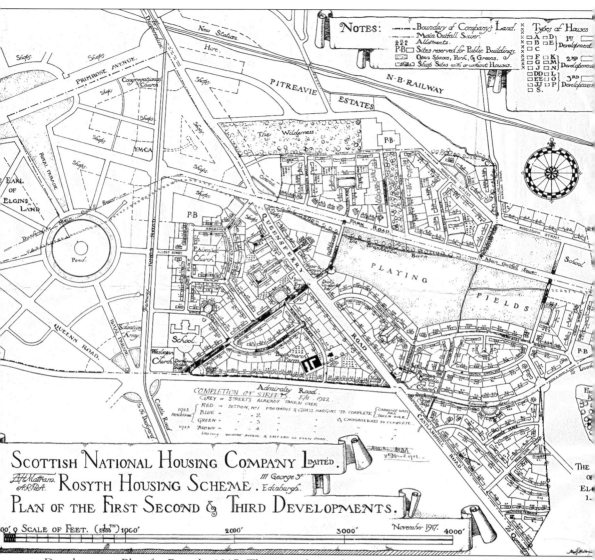

Development Plan for Rosyth, 1917. This map shows the grand plan for Rosyth. By that time, many of the houses were either completed or were being built. It is clearly recognizable as the modern day Rosyth except at the north end of Queensferry Road (where the planned shopping centre became houses) and to the west of King's Road.

Backmarch Road (A1), *c.1920*. This is at its junction with Admiralty Road and shows some of the earliest houses built in Rosyth. The wooden hut is on the site of the present day Wilkies and may have been the temporary premises of the earlier business of Featherstones (see page 62). (Davidson PPC)

Backmarch Crescent (A3), *c.1920*. At its junction with Backmarch Road and again the houses are amongst the earliest in Rosyth. (PPC)

Backmarch Road from Parkgate, *c.1920*. The open space on the right-hand side of the photograph is the site for Rosyth Parish Church. (Valentine PPC)

Findlay Street, *c.1920*. This view is from its junction with Backmarch Road looking north-west towards its junction with Findlay Crescent. (PPC)

Queensferry Road at the Crossroads, *c.1920*. The houses on the left were part of the first phase of development and those on the right were in the second phase. The single storey cottages on the right are the farm cottages of Backmarch Farm (see page 17). The building on the left is the first shop to be built on that corner. This was a chemist's shop before being taken over as a bakery in 1928. It is presently part of Stephen's Bakery. (Valentine PPC)

Admiralty Road at the Crossroads, *c.1920*. This view is from the eastern part of Admiralty Road looking back towards the Crossroads. (RDC PPC)

43

Selvage Street, *c.1920*. Taken from its southern end with the Fairykirk Road junction in the foreground. (PPC)

Parkside Street, Road D. 12, Rosyth

Parkside Street, *c.1920*. The main road in the foreground is Admiralty Road with Parkside Street at the right hand edge. (Valentine PPC)

Middlebank Street, *c.1920*. We have now moved across the Public Park to Middlebank Street, looking north-west to where it joins Woodside Avenue. Burnside Street goes off to the right and Burnside Place to the left. The postcard itself is of some interest as it was published by local newsagent Edwin Reid. (PPC).

East End of Park Road, *c.1920*. The area which is now the Public Park is on the left and the junction with Burnside Place is at the pillar box to the left of centre. When the paddling pool was built in 1938, provision was made to dam the burn to the north of where it passes under Park Road. This allowed water to be taken by pipe to fill the paddling pool on the other side of the road. (PPC)

Holborn Place from the South, *c.1920*. This view is from the Park Road end. (PPC)

Holborn Place from the North, 1931. Unusually, we can date this postcard fairly accurately. It was taken in 1931 and the two girls are Mrs Florence Russell (nee Hutchison) and Jessie Timms. The trees and shrubs have grown somewhat compared to the postcard above and a lamp-post has appeared. (Dunfermline Public Library – Lilywhite PPC)

Cromwell Road from its South End, *c.1930*. As noted in the introduction to this section, work on these houses began in 1921. The area to the left was a spur of the Wilderness Woods and this remained as woodland until the bungalows were built there in the early 1950s. The few trees standing beside the Health Centre are all that now remain of this woodland spur. (PPC)

Road D. 27 and Road D. 31, Rosyth

Woodside Street and Pinkerton Place, *c.1920*. A difficult view to identify. The houses on the extreme left are in Woodside Street (D31) and those in the centre are in Pinkerton Place (D27). The road at the right hand edge is Leslie Road. As there are no houses in Park Road and Leslie Road, the photograph must have been taken before 1921. (Valentine PPC)

Woodside Street, *c.1925*. We move further along Park Road to the bottom of Woodside Street looking north towards Woodside Avenue. (PPC)

Queensferry Road at its north end. On the right are some of the forty houses completed in May 1924. The picture was taken from outside Rosyth Surgery. The bus, car and Belisha beacon suggest that it dates from the late 1930s. (PPC)

General view of Rosyth from Fairykirk, *c.1930*. Admiralty Road is snaking its way through the photograph. The Co-op building at the Crossroads has been erected as has St John and St Columba's RC church and the kiosk at the Crossroads. Note the absence of any buildings on the south side of Admiralty Road from the Crossroads onwards. Just visible in the far distance beside Admiralty Road is the Fleet grounds pavilion with its clock tower. (J.B. White (?) PPC)

Rosyth, East End, from Fairykirk.

General View of East Rosyth from Fairykirk, *c.1930*. In this view, Admiralty Road runs across the foreground with Parkside Street going off to the left and Craig Street to the right. Park Road School has been erected and the Holloway Huts (see page 53) have been demolished. (J.B. White PPC)

Above and below: Rosyth Brickworks, 1918. The Rosyth Brick and Tile Company established a brickworks to the east of Park Road School, no doubt with the aim of supplying bricks for Rosyth houses. They did not have it all their own way as there is a reference in the Dunfermline Press to eight million bricks being delivered to the site from Townhill. The view above is taken from the Inverkeithing Rosyth railway line, which ran to the north of the site. Note the lorry on the left. The view below is of the pit from which the clay was extracted to make the bricks. The men in the foreground are German prisoners of war who were engaged in this work.

Four

The Garden City – Shops

In common with other new communities, the Garden City residents initially had either to go to a neighbouring community (Inverkeithing) for their food and other essentials, or to buy from visiting tradesmen. However, it was not long before businesses were looking to establish themselves in the town. A number of temporary shops were opened, including the Dunfermline Co-operative Society's store at the top of Backmarch Road (in June 1917) and the shopping centre in the Holloway Huts near Park Road School (in 1918). Fraser and Carmichael opened the first of their shops (in the block opposite the Parish Church) at the end of 1917, closely followed by Dick's Co-operative Institutions' permanent store on the opposite corner of Parkgate in February 1918. At the Crossroads, Fairs opened a shop around 1918 and the Dunfermline Co-op opened their department store in December 1920. The shopping centre at the Palace Buildings opened in about 1922.

The temporary Co-op store, *c.1925*. Dunfermline Coop's temporary store at the top of Backmarch Road was opened in June 1917 and in these small premises were grocery, bakery, drapery, boot and butchery shops. This photograph is from the scrapbook of Jimmy Patterson who was very involved with the YMCA Red Triangle Club almost next door to the shops (see page 77). Jimmy is second from the right of the photograph and the others are cryptically named as Cecil, Jaik, Tom and DD.

The temporary Coop store. The store was popularly known as 'The Wee Store', (presumably to distinguish it from the larger Coop store at the Crossroads). This later view was taken around 1951, by which time part of the building was used as a hall which could be hired for parties etc. It was demolished in the 1960s.

East Rosyth from Fairykirk, *c.1925*. This early view of Rosyth shows the huts erected by the firm of Holloway Brothers (who built most of the houses in the Garden City) for their workmen. When this purpose was served, the Scottish National Housing Company obtained permission from the Town Council in 1918 to convert the long rectangular block into about fourteen shops. It was nicknamed 'Arizona' or 'Bond Street' and was in use until about 1926. (PPC)

Fouweathers' Shop, *c.1925*. Mrs Fouweather and her daughter Cissie outside their shop in the Holloway Huts. They later had 'The Wee Shop' at the Palace Buildings.

Dick's Co-op (DCI), *c.1920*. The store was at the corner of Queensferry Road and Parkgate and nowadays is the Forth Bingo and Social Club. The DCI closed down in 1954 and the premises were bought by a Mr Duncan of Townhill and later by William Lows.

Dick's Co-op interior, *c.1920*. A view inside the DCI shop probably of the same date as the one above. Certainly before the days of self-service!

Shops at the Parkgate junction, c.1920. Here we see the DCI open for business but the Fraser and Carmichael block has still to be completed. The building on the extreme left bears the sign 'Rosyth Post Office.' These were temporary premises and the post office later moved round the corner to Parkgate (see page 58). (PPC)

Temporary Premises of the Clydesdale Bank, c.1925. This hut was on the site of the present bank premises across the road from the Parish Church. The temporary premises were opened in 1922 and were to last for some eleven years until a permanent building was opened in 1933. Provost Wyllie of Inverkeithing was the first manager and perhaps he is the bearded gentlemen in the photograph. (Dunfermline Public Library)

Above and below: Shops at the Parkgate Junction. No, this is not a spot the difference competition, but it is interesting to compare these two photographs taken some fifteen years apart. The photograph above includes the temporary Clydesdale Bank premises and probably dates from around 1928. In the photograph below, the permanent bank premises have been erected, the trees have grown substantially, a telephone box has appeared and the car is a later model! (PPCs)

Reids the stationers shop, *c.1930*. This was in the Fraser and Carmichael block of shops (No. 109). The business was owned by two brothers, T. and R. Reid. They started in the Holloway Huts in 1918 and moved to the Palace Buildings in 1926, before finally moving to these premises. They retired from business in 1937 and were succeeded by Messrs T. and S. Jenkins. The shop is now occupied by Goughs the newsagents.

Scotts the Chemists Shop, *c.1934*. This was at No. 115 Queensferry Road, part of the Fraser and Carmichael block of shops. The owner of the business, Mr Henry Scott, who appears in this photograph, died in 1945. The business opened its present premises in the Queens Buildings in 1956. This is now The Gift Shop.

Rosyth Post Office in Parkgate, c.1927. These premises were opened in 1927 and this photograph was probably taken about that time. It was replaced by a new post office at the Crossroads in 1952 and since then has been used as a dentist's surgery.

Aerial View of the Parkgate Area, c.1930. The road across the foreground is Norval Place with Queensferry Road running parallel to it in the centre. The area at the left-hand edge is the site for the Parish Church. The temporary fence surrounding it points to this photograph being taken in 1930, just before building work was under way. The Masonic Hall in Parkgate has been erected, along with the Carnegie Institute.

Dunfermline Co-op's Premises, *c.1925*. We move now to the Crossroads area. On the right are the permanent buildings opened by Dunfermline Co-operative Society Ltd in December 1920. In its early days the hall above was used as a cinema (before the Palace Cinema was operational) and latterly as a dance hall (commonly referred to as 'The Snakepit'). Only recently (1999), the building has been converted into flats. (Lilywhite PPC)

Queensferry Road at the Crossroads, *c.1925*. In 1918, Alex Fair of Inverkeithing was granted a building warrant to erect a shop at the Crossroads, seen here at the right of the photograph. It stands beside Backmarch Cottages, which were demolished some time after the Second World War. (Dunfermline Public Library – J.B. White PPC).

ROSYTH FROM WILDERNESS BRAE,

93082. J.V.

Palace Buildings, *c.1925*. The shops and flats were erected shortly after the Palace Picture House in around 1922. We can date this early view with some accuracy from the fact that the St Andrew and St George Episcopal Church is in course of construction. (Valentine PPC)

Queensferry Road and Aberlour Street, Rosyth.

Palace Buildings, *c.1927*. This slightly later view shows one of the public conveniences erected around 1925/26. This was the 'Ladies' with the equivalent 'Gentlemen' in front of the Goth, just off the right edge of the photograph. The shop to the left of the toilets has a sign 'Home Bakery', which was Woods the Bakers (see page 61). The shop to the right has a sign S. W. Rigdon (who had both bakers and confectionery shops). (PPC)

Woods Home Bakery, c.1930. This is Mrs Wood outside her shop at the Palace Buildings. It was later taken over by Crawfords and is now occupied by Haddows wine merchants.

McPhersons, c.1926. This shop, across the road from the Palace Cinema, sold groceries and provisions. It was later bought by Hays (see page 104), who reconstructed it and added a second storey. It is currently occupied by Razzaques.

Cox's Shop in Parkgate. The shop was round the corner from the main shopping area beside the houses in Parkgate. In the photograph, from left to right, are: Miss M McIvor, (later Mrs McBeth), 'Bubbles' Cox (later Mrs Murphy) and Dorothy Cox (later Mrs Elkan). Miss Dorothy Cox had the shop from 1925 and her sister had a hairdressing business in the back. It was later used as a betting shop (Baines) before being converted to a private house (No.10).

Featherstones, 1935. Another firm to set up business in Rosyth were Featherstones of Rochester in Kent. They operated from temporary premises in Admiralty Road in the early 1920s before building these permanent premises in 1925. Featherstones organized an annual drive for their staff and customers and here we see a party of 115 setting off for Loch Tay in 1935. The business was sold to Lawrie and Wilkie in about 1938. (Photograph by Norval).

Five

The Garden City –
Churches and Schools

The massive influx of population into the area created a need for churches and schools. There were a number of temporary church buildings in the Tin Town area but the Garden City soon replaced Tin Town as the main centre of population. The Scottish Episcopal, Congregational and Presbyterian Churches and the Salvation Army very quickly erected temporary premises in the Garden City. The Wesleyan Methodist, Baptist and Roman Catholic Churches held services in other buildings before going on to establish their own premises. With the exception of the Congregational Church and the Salvation Army, all these bodies had built permanent places of worship by the mid-1930s.

From the outset, pressure on school accommodation was great with children from Tin Town attending schools in neighbouring communities and various temporary schools. The first permanent school to be erected in Rosyth was King's Road School (in 1918), followed by Park Road School in 1922. No sooner were these schools completed than they were full with children brought in from a variety of different kinds of temporary accommodation. A temporary school for Roman Catholic children was replaced with a permanent school (St John's) in 1924. Even with the completion of the permanent schools, a temporary school near King's Road School continued in use and was known as the Third School. This was largely destroyed by fire in 1926 but as it coincided with the closure of the Dockyard and the exodus of a number of families from Rosyth, it was not replaced.

Temporary Episcopal Church. In 1917, St Andrew and St George Scottish Episcopal Church erected this temporary church on the south side of Admiralty Road at the Crossroads. It served them for nine years until their new church in King's Place was opened. The building was then taken over by the British Legion.

Congregational Church. In April 1918 the Congregational Church opened this temporary church on a site at the north end of King's Road. This was remote from the area which had been developed for housing at the time but was possibly with an eye to the future expansion of Rosyth. Sadly their foresight came to nothing as the building was destroyed by fire in 1925. The closure of the Dockyard soon afterwards presumably led to a decision not to replace the building.

Baptist Church. In March 1923 the Baptist Church was opened. The congregation had been formed in 1918, holding their services in one of the schools and later in the YMCA Red Triangle Hut at the top of Backmarch Road (see page 77). This fairly modern view (1975) shows the church and the hall that was added in May 1955 (since replaced with a permanent building).

St Andrew and St George Scottish Episcopal Church. The church was opened in January 1926. The original plans for the church were based on the assumption that the population of Rosyth would rise to about 30,000. The announcement that the Dockyard was to close was made when the church was being built and the plans were curtailed, with an undistinguished western gable end being added instead. Despite this, the church was listed as being of architectural interest (the architect was Sir Ninian Comper). It was demolished in 1986 and the site is now occupied by housing (Mellor Court). (PPC)

St John and St Columba's Roman Catholic Church. The church was opened in October 1926 and as can be seen from this view (taken in 1961), the main entrance was originally in the gable end facing the Crossroads (see also page 71). The roundabout at the Crossroads has taken many forms over the years. This version erected in the early 1950s was probably the grandest of them all. (Dunfermline Public Library – photograph by R Whitehead)

Methodist Church. The Methodist Church was badly affected by the closure of the Dockyard in 1926 with about 90 per cent of its membership moving to the Southern Dockyards. The temporary church and institute in Castle Road was sold and what remained of the congregation obtained the use of the former library building in Backmarch Steading (see page 15). A steady increase in the congregation enabled them to open this church in Parkgate in 1934. The congregation later built a new church (see page 111) and the building in Parkgate is now part of the Bingo premises.

Rosyth Parish Church. The Parish Church obtained a site at the corner of Queensferry Road and Backmarch Road, erecting a hut in 1917. This served as their church until their permanent church building was opened in July 1931. The upper photograph shows the church at the time it was opened. The view below is in the early 1950s when the railings removed during the Second World War had been replaced with a brick wall. (Dunfermline Public Library and Valentine PPC)

PARISH CHURCH, ROSYTH

B 2700

Salvation Army. The Rosyth Corps erected a hut on the south side of Admiralty Road in December 1919. This photograph from 1925 shows the band outside the hall. The Salvation Army also opened a Naval Institute on the east side of Castle Road in January 1920.

Parish Church Choir Outing, *c.1920*. Rev. Guy Scanlan is the minister and amongst the others are Mrs Young and M. Young, Mr & Mrs Lawrie, Miss King, Mr Anderson, Mr David King, Mr McIlroy, Miss J. Bowman, Mr Stewart, Mr Anderson, Mr and Miss McNab, Mrs M. Watson, David Bowan, D. Cairns, Miss L. Simpson, Miss L. McGillivray and the Young brothers.

Rosyth Parish Church Sunday School, *c.1931*. A group of sailors and fishwives, as part of a Kinderspiel presented by the Sunday School. In the back row are Grizel Binnie (third from left), Elspeth McKee (fourth from left) and Mary Gorman (fifth from left). In the middle row are ? Stewart (on the left) and Hetty Syme (fifth from left). In the centre of the group of three, in the front, is Murray Donaldson with Ruth Syme on the right.

Rosyth Parish Church Sunday School, *c.1939*. A later photograph of a Sunday School performance. In the group of pixies at the front are sisters Norah Pollard (second from right) and Audrie Pollard (on the right).

Above and below: King's Road School. This was the first permanent school to be opened in Rosyth. The pressure on school accommodation was such that ten of the classrooms were occupied in April 1918, with the remaining ten being brought into use after the summer holidays, giving accommodation for 1,000 pupils. For some reason the formal opening of the school did not take place until May 1919. The view above probably dates from the 1920s and the one below from the 1930s. Note the outside toilet block. (J.B. White and M.&L. National Series PPCs)

Park Road School. Opened in 1922, the school was immediately filled with pupils who were meeting in temporary accommodation in schools and halls. It had a roll of 750 pupils. An early distant view of the school can be seen on page 53. This view dates from the early 1950s. (Valentine PPC courtesy of St Andrews University Library)

St John's RC School. The last of the permanent pre-war schools to be built in Rosyth. It was opened in August 1924, replacing a temporary school which had been in use since March 1919. It stood beside St John and St Columba's RC Church, seen here on the right of the photograph, and was demolished after the new St John's School was opened in 1988 (see page 124). (J.B. White PPC)

Temporary school class, *c.1919*. The location of the school is not given but the background wall is very similar to those of the original temporary school (later known as the Third School) built close to the site of King's Road School. See the photographs on page 77.

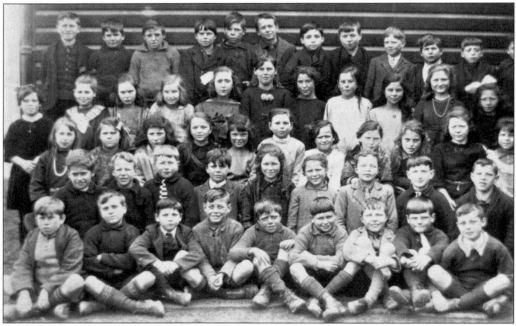

Temporary school class, *c.1920*. At first glance it might seem that this was taken in a gymnasium but on closer inspection the horizontal lines appear to be gaps between the wooden planks of the building.

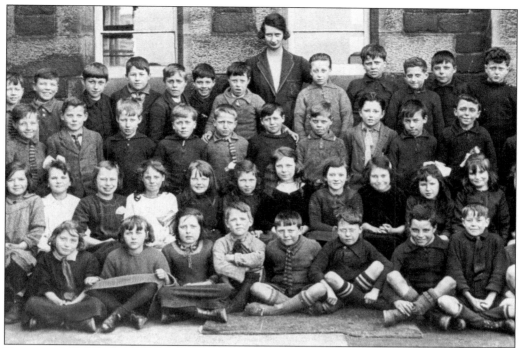

Temporary school class, *c.1920.* Yet another class described as being from one of the temporary Rosyth schools. The school is not identified and the stone wall behind the children is a puzzling feature for a temporary school. Could this be the wall of King's Road School?

King's Road School pupils, 1930. An infant class in costume for a schools festival. Possibly this was the Fife, Kinross and Clackmannanshire Musical Festival held in Kirkcaldy, at which the school won the Folk Dance section. The teacher is Miss M Rennie. In the back row are Ada Burns (fourth from left) and Elspeth McKee (second from right). In the second front row, from left to right, are Ivy Upton, -?-, Rhona Clackson, Isa Lee, Bertha Campbell, -?-, -?-, -?-, -?-, -?- , Muriel McMaster, Jean Fraser,-?-. In the front row are Daisy Cheyne (fourth from left) and Fay Drummond (seventh from left).

King's Road School pupils, *c.1934*. A similar location to the bottom photograph on page 73. The same teacher, Miss M. Rennie, appears in both.

King's Road School pupils, *c.1938*. An older group with a cup. They look very sportily dressed and perhaps this was after a school or inter-school sports competition. In the back row on the right is Jack Deas. In the second back row is ? Johnstone (second from left), Harold Eyddman (second from right) and Willie McReary (on the right). In the second front row are Hughie Taylor (second from left), Davie Crawford (fourth from left) and Duncan Stewart (sixth from left). In the front row are Donald Burns (fourth from left) and ? Cameron (sixth from left). (Photograph by Norval)

Six

The Garden City – Social Life and Leisure

In the 1920s and 1930s, people largely made their own entertainment. There were many clubs and societies formed in Rosyth and the photographs in this section can only give a taste of the wide range of activities open to people in the town. The Carnegie Dunfermline Trust decided that their remit extended to the Rosyth area as part of the enlarged Dunfermline Burgh and Rosyth benefited from this chiefly in the construction of the Carnegie Institute and Rosyth Bowling Green. Convenient to Rosyth were Pitreavie Playing Fields, although Rosyth organisations were also able to use the Fleet grounds. The development of the Public Park in Rosyth was a slow business with some basic levelling work being done in the 1920s, the provision of swings etc. in 1927 and the paddling pool in 1938.

There was a strong temperance movement in the Garden City and attempts to obtain drinks licences were successfully opposed in an effort to keep Rosyth 'dry.' This discouraged the provisions of hotels, public houses, etc. and it was not until 1921 that the first licences were granted – a grocer's licence to Dicks Co-op and a hotel licence to Rosyth Gothenburg Hotel Association.

Above and below: Fancy Dress Carnival, 1920. This was probably the carnival organised by Rosyth Ratepayers Association in June, which a newspaper report describes as 'of rather a small scale but entirely successful.' The proceeds were in aid of the Association and Rosyth Dockyard Brass Band. The photograph above is of the procession in Castle Road (the tram tracks are on the left) and below at the Crossroads when it truly was a crossroads. From this early view it is interesting to note the corner of the temporary Episcopal Church at the left-hand edge, Fairs shop on the right and the first of the shops on the other corner of the Admiralty Road/Queensferry Road junction.

YMCA Red Triangle Club, Backmarch Road. The club was started in 1917 and these premises were opened in March 1918. There was a full time secretary, George Simpson, who can be seen at the back of this group of boys (some of whom are Wolf Cubs). Behind the club hut is a wooden hut which was probably the Third School and beyond that is King's Road School. The photograph was probably taken in the early 1920s (see later photographs on page 102). (J.B. White (?) PPC)

YMCA Red Triangle Club. A formal photograph taken in 1926. Fourth from the left in the second front row is George Simpson and second from the right in the same row is Jimmy Patterson, who later served as club secretary for many years. There is a better view of the 'Third School' in the background. (Photograph by Norval)

Rosyth Bowling Green. This was provided by the Carnegie Dunfermline Trust and opened in 1919. St Andrew and St George Episcopal church (opened in 1926) can be seen in the background, which suggests this photograph was taken in the late 1920s. (J B White ? PPC)

Rosyth Rugby Club, 1921. The club finished champions of the Scottish Midlands League and won the North of Scotland Challenge Cup. Unusually, the names are given on the photograph. From left to right, back row: H.W. Grunsell (Honorary Secretary), W.G. Collins (Committee Member), W. McKee, S. Peel, E. Macdonald, A. Dryden, A. Palmer, F. King and A. Langdon (Committee Members). Middle row: J Sims (Assistant Trainer), H. Parsons, J. Bell, W. Miller, R. Rose, S. Barker, J. Conley, W. Walker, A. King, W. Golding, T. Mills (Trainer). Seated: W. Hoff, C. Birchley, S. Treays, G. Twyman, N. Brown (Captain), R. King, W. Richards, R. Hill. On ground: J. Gwyther and D. Davidson.

Palace Picture House. The cinema was opened in December 1921 and this early photograph probably dates from the mid-1920s. The only shop sign visible is that of Binnings the butcher at the left-hand edge. It was the first cinema in the Dunfermline area to show talking pictures (in 1929) and the first cinemascope film shown was *The Robe* in 1955. It closed as a cinema in June 1971 (see page 112). (Dunfermline Public Library)

St Andrew and St George Church Cricket Club, 1923. A number of the churches had football and cricket teams. The Episcopal Church's cricket team was from left to right, back row: W Cropper (Umpire), E. Walsh, J. Fowler (Committee), P. Pratt, E. Oliver, E. Macdonald; Front row: S. Cordier, C. Carlick, W. McKee, B. Heather (Captain), A. Howse (Vice Captain), F. Philips, J. Oliver.

Rosyth Male Voice Choir, 1924. This was taken to commemorate their success in the Male Voice Choir section of Rosyth Music Festival, held under the auspices of the Rosyth and District Welsh Society. The Festival was held in the Naval Institute in Admiralty Road and was opened by Mr William Adamson, Secretary of State for Scotland. The photograph is taken outside the Baptist Church. At the far left of the back row is Mr David Watson.

Rosyth Garden City Band. This was taken outside the Masonic Hall in Parkgate, probably around 1925. The conductor is Mr Hill. Others included Messrs J. and N. Forster, Mr McIntosh, Mr A. Coombes, Mr Tate and Masters W.G. Coombes and Bob Smith.

Palais de Dance, Park Road. The dance hall was situated where the Good News Supermarket and Wills Garage are today. The building was used as a canteen at Tin Town and when it closed at the end of 1919 the manager, George Mackay, bought the building and re-erected it on this site. He had difficulty in getting a licence and, possibly for this reason, it appears that he sold it. It was opened as a Palais de Dance in October 1922 with a Mr Casey as manager. The building was demolished in 1926 or 1927 to make way for the buildings now on the site. (Dunfermline Public Library)

Carnegie Institute. In 1919 the Carnegie Dunfermline Trust converted two of the Holloway Huts near Park Road School for use as an institute and a hall. (They can be seen on page 53 behind the rectangular block, which was converted into shops). This permanent institute was opened in January 1926, about ten months after the temporary institute was destroyed by fire. This photograph must have been taken within a short time of the opening of the institute. On the right is the Masonic Hall, opened in 1924. (JB White ? PPC)

The library. The library moved from the Backmarch Steading (see page 15) to the Carnegie Institute and opened for business in March 1926. This photograph was probably taken around that time. (Carnegie Dunfermline Trust – photograph by Norval).

The reading room. A room in the Carnegie Institute was given over for reading daily newspapers etc. and seemingly this was quite a popular activity. This is now the new cafe. Again the photograph was probably taken in 1926. (Carnegie Dunfermline Trust – photograph by Norval).

Rosyth Recreation Football Club, 1929. Pictured here is the club's football team for the 1929/30 season.

Rosyth Recreation Cricket Club, 1929. The man seated third from the left holding the cricket ball is Sam Jackson, then of 108 Parkside Street. (Dunfermline Public Library)

The 41st Fife Scout Group, 1935. The Group started in 1925 and was sponsored by Rosyth Parish Church. They moved into their own premises in Backmarch Steading in 1934 and in the war years a second Troop met at the YMCA at the Dockyard. They opened their present headquarters in Woodside Avenue in 1963. This photograph from 1935 shows them receiving the Millar Shield for winning the Rosyth & Inverkeithing Boy Scout Sports. On the left is Mr Alex Millar of Inverkeithing, who donated the trophy, and receiving it on the right is Sam Clouston, Group Scoutmaster of the 41st Fife.

Jubilee bonfire, 1935. The scouts, known for their firelighting abilities, were charged with the task of building this bonfire in the Whinny Hills to mark King George V's Silver Jubilee. On the top are Scouters of the 52nd Fife (Rosyth YMCA) Scout Group – John Wallace, Jimmy Patterson and Andy Wilson. At the bottom is Harold Jackson of the 61st Fife (St John's RC Church) Scout Group.

Pavilion at Pitreavie Playing Fields. Although on the periphery of Rosyth, I could not resist including this early photograph of the pavilion at Pitreavie Playing Fields, which was opened in June 1934. Not many people will remember the distinctive clock tower which was removed after the war. (Carnegie Dunfermline Trust – photograph by Norval)

Rosyth Parish Church Guides, 1938. A group of girl guides from the Parish Church on a trip to the Empire Exhibition at Bellahouston, Glasgow. The Captain in the back row is Miss Moyes, whose father was the headmaster of King's Road School. In the front row, holding her hat, is Elspeth McKee.

The Public Park. A view of Rosyth Public Park from around the early 1930s. The area fenced off in the bottom left hand corner is probably the grounds of the Parkgate Institute. The brickworks' chimneys and Park Road School can be seen in the distance. (M.&L. National Series PPC)

Paddling pool, Rosyth. This might have been taken soon after the pool was completed in 1938 or possibly post-war. The pool was a popular feature of the park during the summer, with model yachts joining the bathers. (J.B. White (?) PPC)

Seven

Greater Rosyth –
The 1940s and 1950s

During the late 1920s and for most of the 1930s there was very little house building in Rosyth and the town boundaries did not change to any extent. As the threat of war approached and the Dockyard was re-opened, there was a great deal of development in Rosyth and in the Dockyard. The term 'Greater Rosyth' might seem somewhat grand but I simply use it to indicate that in this (and subsequent) sections we are looking wider than the original Garden City of Rosyth.

In 1939 the Town Council completed the Wemyss Street/Nelson Street housing scheme and the Scottish National Housing Company built the houses in King's Road. In 1941/42 the Admiralty were responsible for the building of a major new housing estate south of Admiralty Road (commonly referred to as 'Dollytown'). As the war drew to a close, there were fears that the Dockyard would again be closed. In fact, during the late 1940s and 1950s a considerable amount of development work was carried out in the Dockyard and more houses were erected in Rosyth – the Burnside estate, the first part of the Camdean estate and married quarters at the Dockyard.

Primrose Camp. An anti-aircraft battery was sited to the west of Primrose Farm as part of the Forth defences. For a short time after the war, the camp was used as a re-training centre for those who were to be demobbed. It closed down in about 1947 and for a number of years part of it was used as a training centre for Fife Army Cadets. This photograph (in 1974) is taken from the junction of Primrose Lane and Brankholm Brae. Little now remains of the camp other than the boundary fence, foundations of buildings and the Commanding Officer's bungalow, which is still in use.

Winston Churchill at Rosyth Dockyard, 1940. Winston Churchill was no stranger to Rosyth having visited the Dockyard in 1912 and 1913 when he was First Lord of the Admiralty. Here we see him at Rosyth as Prime Minister in the early days of the Second World War. (Courtesy of the Imperial War Museum, London)

The Battleship King George V, 1940. This was probably taken during Winston Churchill's visit to the Dockyard as another photograph (not included in the book) shows Winston Churchill addressing this ship's company. The Dockyard workshops and the buildings of HMS *Caledonia* can be seen in the background. (Courtesy of the Imperial War Museum, London)

British Sailors' Society Hostel, 1941. The occasion was the formal opening of the hostel in Castle Road. The Commander-in-Chief, Vice Admiral Sir Charles Gordon Ramsey, is presented with a golden key by Lord Elgin, Lord Lieutenant of Fife. The hostel had 52 bedrooms with dining, reading and recreation rooms. The building is now the Forth Club. (Courtesy of the Imperial War Museum, London)

King George VI at Rosyth, 1941. According to a Press account, he visited two ships in the course of his visit, one of which was HMS *Prince of Wales*. The other (see below) was probably HMS *Hood*. This was one of three visits which the King made to Rosyth during the war. On this occasion he presented medals to eleven men, including three Norwegian sailors. (Courtesy of the Imperial War Museum, London)

King George VI at Rosyth, 1941. He is seen here with Admiral Sir Charles Gordon Ramsey in March 1941. From the Letters HO at the right edge of the photograph, it appears that he was leaving HMS *Hood*. (Courtesy of the Imperial War Museum, London)

King George VI inspecting the Dockyard Home Guard, 1941. The Dockyard had its own Home Guard Battalion separate from the Dunfermline/Rosyth Home Guard. (Courtesy of the Imperial War Museum, London)

Dollytown, viewed from Castlandhill. Many of the men brought from the Southern Dockyards in the early days of the war had to live in Edinburgh because of the shortage of housing. The Dollytown scheme (and a scheme at Brucefield), were built in the early 1940s to provide additional housing for Dockyard workers. This view taken in April 1949 gives some idea of the layout of the scheme. Castlandhill Road is just visible at the extreme right hand edge and at the left hand edge (in the area now occupied by the Camdean Filling Station) is a temporary army camp. (Photograph by R.M. Adam courtesy of St Andrews University Library)

Rosyth Dockyard November, 1943. This view from one of the cranes shows the battleship HMS *Duke of York* in No. 1 Dock nearest the camera, HMS *Berwick* in No. 2 Dock and HMS *Liverpool* in No. 3 Dock. The RN and RM Canteen is in the foreground. (Courtesy of the Imperial War Museum, London)

The Aircraft Carrier HMS *Indomitable*, 1944. She is manoeuvring in the basin before entering No. 2 Dock. Note the Avenger aircraft on her deck. (Courtesy of the Imperial War Museum, London)

The Flag Mast in the Dockyard, 1944. This was outside the Admiral Superintendent's offices. Mr J. Henderson, head messenger, is attending to the flags. The nameplates are of ships from the German fleet broken up at Rosyth in the 1930s. (Courtesy of the Imperial War Museum, London)

The Early Shift Leaving the Dockyard, 1944. The Dockyard relied heavily on women workers during the war. (Courtesy of the Imperial War Museum, London)

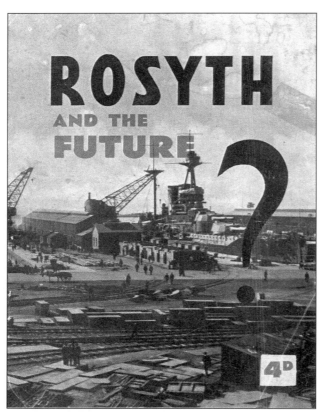

Rosyth and the Future, 1946. As the Second World War drew to a close, the Trade Unions were very active in trying to counter any move to close the Dockyard. This is the front page of a booklet published in February 1946 to publicize the case for retaining the Dockyard.

Salvation Army Hall, Backmarch Road, 1973. The Salvation Army previously had a hall in Admiralty Road (see page 68) but this closed down. The Corps was re-established and in 1946 erected a hut at the top of Backmarch Road on the site of the former Red Triangle Club (see page 77). The hut was replaced in 1966 with this one brought from Dundee.

Prefabs in Camdean. The pressures on housing accommodation led to the provision of temporary prefabricated houses (prefabs) in many parts of the country. A group of fifty were built in Camdean in 1948/49. This later view (1971) shows some of the prefabs in Camdean Crescent. The scheme was demolished in 1975 and in 1978 the site was sold off as individual feus for private houses.

Park Road (West) Residents. In front of the prefabs in Park Road (West) are a number of local residents, including David and Mina Butchart (second and third from the left).

Queensferry Road at Parkgate. This view from around 1950 shows a few changes from earlier views (see pages 56 and 57). The trees have grown to such an extent that the ones in front of the shops have been severely pruned. One of the shops (No. 113) has been taken over by Arneils the hairdresser. The DCI is still trading but not for much longer as the business closed in 1954. (Valentine PPC courtesy of St Andrews University Library).

Parkgate Institute. This view from about 1951 shows a marked improvement over the 1926 view (page 81) and, indeed, the present view! (Valentine PPC courtesy of St Andrews University Library)

Queensferry Road. This view from about 1951 looks towards the Parish Church (on the left) and the junction with Parkside Street (in the centre). The block of houses towards the right is of particular interest. The middle two (with the combined porch) were modified in 1917 to be used as offices for the Housing Company's Clerk of Works. In 1919 they were taken over by the police for use as living accommodation for two married constables and as a police station. (Valentine PPC courtesy of St Andrews University Library)

Crowning of the Gala Queen, 1952. In 1950 Rosyth Parish Church promoted a Gala Week, which ran for many years. The 1952 Gala Queen, Margaret Allan, (later Mrs Bucke) was crowned by Mrs Crombie, wife of the Admiral Superintendent of the Dockyard. The attendants are listed in the *Press* as Catherine Edwards and Maureen Daniels (Maids ofHonour), Christine Sherman and Eileen Bowman (Train Bearers), Gordon Craig (Crown Bearer) and John Scott (Herald). Duncan Munro and Gordon Scott presented bouquets to Mrs Crombie and the Gala Queen.

Coronation Celebrations, 1953. Rosyth joined in the Coronation celebrations in June 1953 with a number of street parties. This one was held for children in Findlay Street.

Camdean Primary School. The first new school in Rosyth for many years was opened in September 1953 (the infant department having opened the previous year). This is a view from Admiralty Road. The Camdean prefab site can be seen in the distance.

Naval Married Quarters in Cunningham Road, 1953. The increasing importance of Rosyth as a naval base led to the building of married quarters for officers and ratings. This view from Hilton Road shows the early stages of the construction of the Cunningham Road married quarters with numbers 1-9 on the left and 2-8 in the middle. The Dockyard College buildings are on the right and Castlandhill is in the background.

Naval Married Quarters in Somerville Road, 1954. This view of work in progress is from the south end with No. 5 on the left and the gable end of No. 8 on the right.

Aerial view of Rosyth, 1955. This gives some idea of the extent to which Rosyth had developed by April 1955. It is possible to pick out many of the housing schemes, shops, schools etc., which have been referred to in this and earlier sections of this book. For those who need help in orientating themselves, the road running parallel to the left hand edge is King's Road. Pitreavie Castle is at the top while Castlandhill Farm and the Officers Club in Castle Road are at the bottom. (British Crown Copyright/MOD)

Model of the Royal Yacht *Britannia*, 1954. This model was part of the Dunfermline Week procession in June 1954. The globe depicted the route of the royal tour after Queen Elizabeth's Coronation in 1953.

Rosyth Youth Orchestra, *c.1956*. The orchestra was drawn from pupils of Park Road School. It grew out of an initiative by Fife Education Authority and the Carnegie Dunfermline Trust to teach pupils to play the violin. On the left is the conductor Mrs Iris Atkinson. Next to her in the back row is Connie Hubbucks and also in that row is Ronnie Ellis (fifth from right) and Joan Scott (second from right). In the front row (from the left) are Alexis Hutton, -?-, -?-, Diane Bowman, Johnny Bell, -?-, Billy McSweeney, John Evans, Mark Rennie and John Blench. (Dunfermline Press)

Above and below: Rosyth Bowling Club. The bowling green was opened in 1919 (see the earlier photograph on page 78) but it was many years before a permanent clubhouse was provided. The cost was met by the Carnegie Dunfermline Trust and here we see the new clubhouse when it was officially opened on 28 May 1956. In the photograph below, from left to right: Bob Campbell (Assistant Secretary of the Carnegie Dunfermline Trust), John Fraser (Architect), Andrew Blair (President of Rosyth Bowling Club), Ord Cunningham (Chairman of the Carnegie Dunfermline Trust), Provost Gellatly and Bob Meek (Vice Chairman of Rosyth Bowling Club). (Carnegie Dunfermline Trust – photographs by Norval)

A class from Camdean School, c.1956. Most of the children were founder pupils who started in the infant school in 1952. From left to right, back row: Brian Cuthbertson, Alex McDonough, Billy Houston, Philip Simpson, Martin Rogers, Peter Lee, Stuart Hunter, David Underhay, Michael Douglas, Eric Harding, Warren Gundry, Donald Hunter, William McMaster, Sandy Webster, Angus Mair, Billy Ansett. Middle row: Pamela Sands, Patricia Flintham, Maureen Clark, Carol Thorn, Dorothy Fletcher, Valerie Brook, Irene Jeffries, Elizabeth Yates, Helen Bogey, Nancy Handley, Eve Tabb, Doreen Fernie. Front row: Rosalind Russell, Glenda Eaton, Rona Sands, Marion McBeth, Rosaline Russell, Jean Johnson, Eleanor Fitzpatrick, Anne Henderson, Sheila Corkin.

Apprentices Hostel. A hostel for Dockyard apprentices was opened in December 1956 at the junction of Castle and Hilton Roads. In more recent times it was used as a Naval Families Centre. Currently (autumn 1999) it is being refurbished for use as a community resource centre. (This photograph was taken in 1978)

Queens Buildings. In 1954, businessmen with premises in the Palace Buildings combined together to build a new suite of shops on vacant ground across the road. This was named 'Queens Buildings' and was opened towards the end of 1956. As can be seen from the photograph, Messrs Smith, Hatch and Hope all opened businesses in the new premises and were joined by Scotts the Chemists, who had premises near the Clydesdale Bank. Hays shop on the right is the former McPhersons shop (see page 61). This photograph was taken in May 1958 by J. Wright. (Dunfermline Public Library).

Rosyth Pipe Band, 1957. The band outside the Carnegie Institute.

Dockyard cash office, 1957. There was increased optimism about the future of the Dockyard in the late 1950s with plenty of work in hand and new buildings erected to replace temporary wartime structures. This is the newly completed cash office in November 1957.

EEM Workshop, Rosyth Dockyard, 1958. Another new building was the EEM workshop, pictured here in July 1958 as it was nearing completion. It was formally opened by the First Sea Lord, Lord Mountbatten, when he visited the Dockyard in April 1959.

Aerial View of West Rosyth, July 1958. In the foreground is Park Road (West) and Camdean Crescent, showing the prefab site and the Blackburn and Millar space saving houses erected by the Town Council in the early1950s. Camdean School is in the bottom right hand corner. The burn between King's Road and the Palace has still to be culverted and Elder Place has not yet been built. The bungalows are gradually making their way along Woodside Avenue. Wesley House (Wilderness Cottage) can be seen at the end of Woodside Avenue while Rosyth Bowling Green, the Goth and the new Queens Buildings stand out in the right centre. (British Crown Copyright/MOD).

Eight

Greater Rosyth – The 1960s and 1970s

Probably the most significant event of the two decades was the opening of the Forth Road Bridge in September 1964. This made the Dunfermline area more attractive for business and for commuters. It was certainly a period of further expansion and development of the Dockyard and the town of Rosyth. In the 1960s, houses were built in Elder Place and in Camdean and in the 1970s the redevelopment of the Dollytown area started, more naval married quarters were built off Castle Road and the Whinnyburn estate was built. In the early 1960s the Lyle & Scott factory was built in Primrose Lane and some years later an industrial estate was opened up beside it.

Among the new buildings opened in Rosyth were the Civil Service Sports Centre, the new Methodist Church, the fire station in Castle Road, Camdean Community Centre and new premises for the Dockyard Club.

Dual carriageway to Dunfermline, 1961. Taken in February before work started on the construction of the approach roads to the Forth Road Bridge. This is now the site of the Pitreavie roundabout.

Admiralty Road, 1961. The road to Inverkeithing before the Forth Road approaches were built. To the right is the junction with Fairykirk Road and in the background are the buildings connected with Rosyth Quarry.

Elder Place, *c.1961*. Houses being erected on the east side of Elder Place. On the extreme left is Wesley House (see page 18). (Photograph by David Henderson)

Elder Place, *c.1961*. The building of the maisonettes. (Photograph by David Henderson)

The Halt Railway Bridge, 1968. Work is in progress to widen the bridge to its present width. At that time the main traffic flow was down Queensferry Road but this was changed as part of the works to make King's Road the main through road. The present double roundabout was added some years later.

Civil Service Sports Centre. This new clubhouse for the Civil Service Sports Association was opened in October 1968. The previous clubhouse had been a temporary building in McGrigor Road. This photograph was taken in September 1973.

Rosyth Halt, 1969. The roadworks are nearing completion although the Rosyth sign has still to be repositioned! The petrol filling station site is now occupied by Tescos. The present day Cleos can be seen below the Rosyth sign but at this time was known as The Golden Age.

Methodist Church, 1970. In 1969 the Methodist Church sold their church premises in Parkgate (see page 66) to William Lows. They demolished their Wesley House premises at the corner of Queensferry Road and Woodside Avenue (see page 18) and erected this new church which was opened in December 1970.

The Palace Cinema, 1971. The cinema closed its doors in June 1971, almost fifty years after it opened (this *Press* photograph marks the occasion). The building lay empty for some years and is now a public house known as 'Visions.' (An earlier photograph appears on page 79). (*Dunfermline Press*).

Dollytown, 1973. Taken from the western end of Fraser Road looking north over Pound Road and Churchill Road. The Second World War air raid shelter in the foreground could almost have been designed to fit in with the architectural style of the Dollytown housing! At this time, work was under way on redeveloping the eastern side of Dollytown.

Dockyard Club, 1976. The Rosyth Dockyard Workers' Recreation Club was formed in January 1916 and met in temporary premises in Castle Road and Admiralty Road until these new premises were built in 1936. They were later extended in 1940. Only a few months after this photograph was taken the premises were destroyed by fire. New premises were opened on the same site in December 1977. The club has since closed and the premises have been taken over as a public house called 'The Yard.'

Rosyth Fire Station. The fire station in Wood Road in the Dockyard was replaced at the end of 1976 with this new building in Castle Road. Some of the last Dollytown houses can be seen on either side of the station.

Rosyth Palace, 1975. We close this section by having a look at changes in shopping provision in Rosyth. Compare this and the following photographs with those in Section 4 (page 56 onwards). Here, the Palace Cinema is still lying disused after it was closed in 1971. Shops on either side are occupied by Smiths the butcher, Hills dry cleaning, Thomsons the hairdresser and Burts' corner shop.

Palace Buildings, 1978. All but one of the shops in this slightly later photograph have changed their use or ownership in the period up to 1999, the exception being Watsons the bookmakers. The shop second from the right end was occupied by Margaret Langley with the Dunfermline City Bakery having the corner shop.

Palace Buildings, 1978. The two shops at the left-hand edge which are not readily identifiable are the Dunfermline City Bakery and Tazioli's sweet shop. The Palace Fish Restaurant was run by Donald Tazioli, hence the name 'Donald's' on the adjoining shop. This was opened to provide additional seating accommodation. By the time this photograph was taken, the adjoining shop had been taken over by Jarvis as a fruit and vegetable shop.

Wills Garage, 1975. A reminder of the days when Wills operated a petrol filling station as part of the garage premises. Unfortunately, the price of the petrol is not displayed.

Queens Buildings, 1979. There have been a few changes of ownership since the buildings were opened in 1956 (see page 104) with only Scotts and Smith's shops remaining. Hatch's shop has been taken over by R. S. McColls and the Dunfermline Building Society have taken over Hope's shop. This is much as it looks today, apart from the Trustees Savings Bank being in place of Smiths.

Queensferry Road at Parkgate, 1979. Moving down the road there are again a number of changes in the shops (see page 56, 57 and 96). The Gift Shop has replaced Scotts the Chemists at No. 115, Harvey's electrical shop has taken over from Arneils at No. 113, Elders have replaced Reids at No. 109, Browns have opened a fish shop at No. 107 and Junior Smith has taken over Fraser's shop on the corner.

Nine

Recent Times –
The 1980s and 1990s

The last twenty years have seen many changes in Rosyth. Compared to previous decades, there has been very little new public sector housing but private house builders have come to the fore with the development of a number of small estates in different parts of the town. The significance of the Dockyard as an employer has diminished as the size of the Royal Navy has decreased. The Dockyard has changed from a public sector organization to one under private management, and finally to a private company. The Dockyard has sought other outlets for its expertise to try to offset the reduction in naval work.

At one time there was little in the way of employment in Rosyth outside the retail sector but with the establishment of the industrial estates at Primrose and Pitreavie and the location of other major offices and factories on the periphery – the Card (Visa) Centre, Dunfermline Building Society, Sky and Lexmark – there is now a wider range of employment opportunities. The fact that Rosyth was part of the Burgh of Dunfermline and not a burgh in its own right meant that there was little in the way of public buildings in Rosyth. To some extent that too has changed with an additional community centre in Primrose Lane, the establishment of the social work offices and health centre in Park Road and the provision of a resource centre in Granville Way. The long awaited library also became a reality.

In this section I have deliberately not featured these major new developments which are part of the present day Rosyth. Rather, I have concentrated on some of the buildings which had to be demolished and land which had to be given up to allow these developments to proceed.

King's Road/Park Road Junction, 1980. Taken shortly before the present roundabout was constructed at the junction.

Chart Depot, Castle Road. This was one of the original temporary buildings associated with the early days of the Dockyard. For many years it served as a club for Dockyard workers and ended its day as the Dockyard's Chart Depot. The Depot moved to new premises within the Dockyard at the end of 1980 and the building was demolished some time after that. It stood in front of what was then the NAAFI supermarket, hence the sign. (This photograph was taken in July 1974.)

Park Lea housing development, 1981. This was the first of a number of small private housing estates to be developed in Rosyth. This view is taken along the newly constructed access road with the Army Cadet Force's hut at the left-hand edge.

Park Lea housing development, 1981. This view into the site shows the backs of houses in Burnside Crescent on the left and the motorway on the right.

Park Road at its Junction with Parkgate, 1981. On the left hand side of the photograph is the area on which the social work offices now stand. The building of the offices began later in the year.

King's Road, 1982. An unusual sight as these abnormal loads made their way from the Dockyard to Mossmorran via King's Road.

Wemyss Court, 1983. Felling of trees in the western part of the Wilderness Woods to make way for the Wemyss Court private housing development. This view looks east towards the access to the estate from Wemyss Street.

Wemyss Court, 1984. Work under way on the building of the estate. This is taken from a slightly different angle but is again looking east towards the Wemyss Street access.

The east end of Woodside Avenue, 1984. This was taken just as work was commencing on the building of the small group of private houses at the junction of Woodside Avenue and Middlebank Street. Part of the site had previously been used as a garage site.

Granville Way, 1986. A start is made on the private housing development behind the fire station. The old Pound Road is in the foreground. In the distance are houses in Hudson Road.

Mossbank housing estate, 1986. Work begins on the Mossbank estate with the line of the access road shown and some earthmoving under way. The houses visible through the trees are the newly built houses at the Woodside Avenue/Middlebank Street junction.

Mossbank housing estate, 1988. Some twenty months later, the houses are springing up. This is a view from the west end of the site looking towards Burnside Street. The half-built houses in the foreground are Nos 33 and 34.

St John's RC Primary School, 1988. This was taken shortly after the new school in Heath Road was opened, replacing the original school in Crossroads Place (see page 71).

The Woodlands. The topmost section of this field became the site for the Woodlands private housing development in 1989. The houses shown here are in Wemyss Street. This photograph was taken in 1978.

The Byres, 1990. A view of the site cleared for the construction of the Byres housing development. The building on the left is Primrose Farmhouse (see page 18). The houses in the background are in Syme Place.

Fleet grounds pavilion, 1995. This view is from the south with the Glasgow Road on the other side of the pavilion. The pavilion was demolished only a few months after this photograph was taken to make way for the first phase of the Lexmark development.

Pitreavie Castle. At the end of 1995 the Maritime Headquarters at Pitreavie Castle closed. This later view (January 1998) shows the castle on the left with some of the associated offices and accommodation blocks. Shortly afterwards, all of these buildings (with the exception of the castle) were demolished. The buildings were of a very distinctive light green colour.

HMS *Scotia*, 1995. These buildings which stood on the north side of the access road to Pitreavie Castle were the home of HMS *Scotia*, part of the Royal Naval Reserve. They too were demolished in 1998.

Officers Club, Castle Road. This building was the last of the H-shaped blocks that ran up the east side of Castle Road in the early days of the Dockyard (see page 32). For many years it was used as a club for Naval Officers and latterly was a social club, The Jutland Club. The club closed down in 1995 and in November of that year the building was destroyed by fire. The site is now being developed for private housing. In the distance is the clock tower on Pease Hill, erected in 1939 for the benefit of the sailors taking part in sports on the Fleet grounds. (This photograph was taken in September 1973 before the Sherbrooke Road estate was built on the west side of Castle Road.)

HMS *Cochrane*. The entrance gate to HMS *Cochrane* and all the buildings were demolished in 1998 to allow this site to be redeveloped as part of the Europarc proposals. Also demolished was the Naval Store building in the background on the right (see page 34). This photograph was taken in 1978.

The entrance to the Dockyard (as in May 1978). The bus stance on the left was opened in November 1969. Behind the bus stance are the naval store offices. In the centre is the main office building and cash office. In 1998 a roundabout was constructed outside the Dockyard gates to provide access to the new Europarc development.

Rosyth Station ticket office. It is perhaps fitting to end this book with a photograph of a building which has been a familiar landmark in Rosyth for many years. The station ('Rosyth Halt' in those days) was opened at the beginning of 1918 and the ticket office probably dates back to then. Rosyth became an unmanned station some years ago and the ticket office was demolished in July 1999 when work began on the reconstruction of the station.